Hiking Log

The Publisher: Wandering Walks of Wonder Publishing

Kansas City, MO 64118

USA

Website: www.wanderwalksofwonder.com

ISBN-13: 978-1502363770

ISBN-10: 1502363771

Insights, thoughts and feelings:

Date:	Time:	Location & Trail Name:	Distance:
Weather:	Type of Hike: Light Moderate Strenuous		Companions:

The sights, sounds, and smells of this hike:

I have two doctors, my left leg and my right.
~ G.M. Trevelyan

Insights, thoughts and feelings:

Date:	Time:	Location & Trail Name:	Distance:
Weather:	Type of Hike:		Companions:

Weather icons: ☀ ⛅ 🌧 🌨

Type of Hike: Light   Moderate   Strenuous

The sights, sounds, and smells of this hike:

_____

_____

_____

_____

_____

_____

_____

_____

_____

_____

_____

_____

You need special shoes for hiking — and a bit of a special soul as well.

~ Terri Guillemets

Insights, thoughts and feelings:

Date:	Time:	Location & Trail Name:	Distance:
Weather: ☀ ⛅ 🌧 🌨	Type of Hike: Light Moderate Strenuous		Companions:

The sights, sounds, and smells of this hike:

_____

_____

_____

_____

_____

_____

_____

_____

_____

_____

_____

Returning home is the most difficult part of long-distance hiking; You have grown outside the puzzle and your piece no longer fits.
~ Cindy Ross

Insights, thoughts and feelings:

Date:	Time:	Location & Trail Name:	Distance:
Weather:	Type of Hike: Light Moderate Strenuous		Companions:

The sights, sounds, and smells of this hike:

_____

_____

_____

_____

_____

_____

_____

_____

_____

_____

_____

Today is your day! Your mountain is waiting.

So… get on your way.

~ Dr. Seuss

Insights, thoughts and feelings:

Date:	Time:	Location & Trail Name:	Distance:
Weather: ☀ ⛅ 🌧 🌨	Type of Hike: Light Moderate Strenuous		Companions:

The sights, sounds, and smells of this hike:

_____

_____

_____

_____

_____

_____

_____

_____

_____

_____

In the mountains there are only two grades: You can either do it, or you can't.

~ Rusty Baille

Insights, thoughts and feelings:

Date:	Time:	Location & Trail Name:	Distance:
Weather:	Type of Hike: Light Moderate Strenuous		Companions:

The sights, sounds, and smells of this hike:

_____

_____

_____

_____

_____

_____

_____

_____

_____

_____

_____

> *May your trails be crooked, winding, lonesome, dangerous, leading to the most amazing view. May your mountains rise into and above the clouds.*
> *~ Edward Abbey*

Insights, thoughts and feelings:

Date:	Time:	Location & Trail Name:	Distance:
Weather: ☀ ⛅ 🌧 🌨	Type of Hike: Light Moderate Strenuous		Companions:

The sights, sounds, and smells of this hike:

_____

_____

_____

_____

_____

_____

_____

_____

_____

_____

_____

Study nature, love nature, stay close to nature. It will never fail you.

~ Frank Lloyd Wright

Insights, thoughts and feelings:

Date:	Time:	Location & Trail Name:	Distance:
Weather:	Type of Hike: Light Moderate Strenuous		Companions:

The sights, sounds, and smells of this hike:

_____
_____
_____
_____
_____
_____
_____
_____
_____
_____

> *I see my path, but I don't know where it leads. Not knowing where I'm going is what inspires me to travel it.*
> *~ Rosalia de Castro*

Insights, thoughts and feelings:

Date:	Time:	Location & Trail Name:	Distance:

Weather:	Type of Hike:			Companions:
☀ ⛅ 🌧 🌨	Light	Moderate	Strenuous	

The sights, sounds, and smells of this hike:

_____

_____

_____

_____

_____

_____

_____

_____

_____

_____

_____

> *Now I see the secret of making the best person, it is to grow in the open air and to eat and sleep with the earth.*
> *~ Walt Whitman*

Insights, thoughts and feelings:

Date:	Time:	Location & Trail Name:	Distance:
Weather:	Type of Hike: Light Moderate Strenuous		Companions:

The sights, sounds, and smells of this hike:

_____

_____

_____

_____

_____

_____

_____

_____

_____

_____

Take only pictures; leave only footprints.

~ Anonymous

Insights, thoughts and feelings:

Date:	Time:	Location & Trail Name:	Distance:
Weather:	Type of Hike: Light Moderate Strenuous		Companions:

The sights, sounds, and smells of this hike:

_____

_____

_____

_____

_____

_____

_____

_____

_____

_____

_____

> *Only those who will risk going too far can possibly*
> *find out how far they can go.*
> *~ T.S. Eliot*

Insights, thoughts and feelings:

Date:	Time:	Location & Trail Name:	Distance:
Weather: ☀ ⛅ 🌧 🌨	Type of Hike: Light Moderate Strenuous		Companions:

The sights, sounds, and smells of this hike:

_____

_____

_____

_____

_____

_____

_____

_____

_____

_____

_____

Thoughts come clearly while one walks.
~ Thomas Mann

Insights, thoughts and feelings:

Date:	Time:	Location & Trail Name:	Distance:
Weather: ☀ ⛅ 🌧 🌨	Type of Hike: Light Moderate Strenuous		Companions:

The sights, sounds, and smells of this hike:

_____

_____

_____

_____

_____

_____

_____

_____

_____

_____

_____

It is not the mountain we conquer but ourselves.
-- Edmund Hillary

Insights, thoughts and feelings:

Date:	Time:	Location & Trail Name:	Distance:
Weather: ☀ ⛅ 🌧 🌨	Type of Hike: Light Moderate Strenuous		Companions:

The sights, sounds, and smells of this hike:

_____

_____

_____

_____

_____

_____

_____

_____

_____

_____

_____

_____

If you can find a path with no obstacles, it probably doesn't lead anywhere.

~ Frank A. Clark

Insights, thoughts and feelings:

Date:	Time:	Location & Trail Name:	Distance:
Weather: ☀ ⛅ 🌧 🌨	Type of Hike: Light　Moderate　Strenuous		Companions:

The sights, sounds, and smells of this hike:

_____

_____

_____

_____

_____

_____

_____

_____

_____

_____

_____

I only went out for a walk and finally concluded to stay out till sundown, for going out, I found, was really going in. ~John Muir

Insights, thoughts and feelings:

Date:	Time:	Location & Trail Name:	Distance:
Weather:	Type of Hike:		Companions:
	Light Moderate Strenuous		

The sights, sounds, and smells of this hike:

_____

_____

_____

_____

_____

_____

_____

_____

_____

_____

_____

Adopt the pace of nature: her secret is patience.

~Ralph Waldo Emerson

Insights, thoughts and feelings:

Date:	Time:	Location & Trail Name:	Distance:
Weather: ☀ ⛅ 🌧 🌨	Type of Hike: Light Moderate Strenuous		Companions:

The sights, sounds, and smells of this hike:

_____

_____

_____

_____

_____

_____

_____

_____

_____

_____

_____

Climb up on some hill at sunrise. Everybody needs perspective once in a while, and you'll find it there.

~Robb Sagendorph

Insights, thoughts and feelings:

Date:	Time:	Location & Trail Name:	Distance:
Weather:	Type of Hike: Light Moderate Strenuous		Companions:

The sights, sounds, and smells of this hike:

Solvitur ambulando, St. Jerome was fond of saying.
To solve a problem, walk around.

~Gregory McNamee

Insights, thoughts and feelings:

Date:	Time:	Location & Trail Name:	Distance:
Weather:	Type of Hike: Light Moderate Strenuous		Companions:

The sights, sounds, and smells of this hike:

_____

_____

_____

_____

_____

_____

_____

_____

_____

_____

_____

A pedestrian is someone who thought there were a couple of gallons left in the tank.

~Author Unknown

Insights, thoughts and feelings:

Date:	Time:	Location & Trail Name:	Distance:
Weather:	Type of Hike: Light Moderate Strenuous		Companions:

The sights, sounds, and smells of this hike:

_____

_____

_____

_____

_____

_____

_____

_____

_____

_____

_____

Make your feet your friend.

~J.M. Barrie

Insights, thoughts and feelings:

Date:	Time:	Location & Trail Name:	Distance:
Weather: ☀ ⛅ 🌧 🌨	Type of Hike: Light Moderate Strenuous		Companions:

The sights, sounds, and smells of this hike:

_____

_____

_____

_____

_____

_____

_____

_____

_____

_____

_____

The best remedy for a short temper is a long walk.

~Jacqueline Schiff

Insights, thoughts and feelings:

Date:	Time:	Location & Trail Name:	Distance:
Weather:	Type of Hike: Light Moderate Strenuous		Companions:

The sights, sounds, and smells of this hike:

_____

_____

_____

_____

_____

_____

_____

_____

_____

_____

_____

We live in a fast-paced society. Walking slows us down.

~Robert Sweetgall

Insights, thoughts and feelings:

Date:	Time:	Location & Trail Name:	Distance:
Weather: ☀ ⛅ 🌧 🌨	Type of Hike: Light Moderate Strenuous		Companions:

The sights, sounds, and smells of this hike:

_____

_____

_____

_____

_____

_____

_____

_____

_____

_____

_____

_____

> *If I could not walk far and fast, I think I should*
> *just explode and perish.*
>
> *~Charles Dickens*

Insights, thoughts and feelings:

Date:	Time:	Location & Trail Name:	Distance:
Weather: ☀ ⛅ 🌧 🌨	Type of Hike: Light Moderate Strenuous		Companions:

The sights, sounds, and smells of this hike:

_____
_____
_____
_____
_____
_____
_____
_____
_____
_____
_____

I stroll along serenely, with my eyes, my shoes, my
rage, forgetting everything.
~Pablo Neruda

Insights, thoughts and feelings:

Date:	Time:	Location & Trail Name:	Distance:
Weather:	Type of Hike: Light Moderate Strenuous		Companions:

The sights, sounds, and smells of this hike:

_____

_____

_____

_____

_____

_____

_____

_____

_____

_____

_____

Hiking is the best workout!... You can hike for three hours and not even realize you're working out. And, hiking alone lets me have some time to myself.
~Jamie Luner

Insights, thoughts and feelings:

Date:	Time:	Location & Trail Name:	Distance:
Weather:	Type of Hike: Light Moderate Strenuous		Companions:

The sights, sounds, and smells of this hike:

_____

_____

_____

_____

_____

_____

_____

_____

_____

_____

*Thousands of tired, nerve-shaken, over-civilized
people are beginning to find out going to the
mountains is going home; that wilderness is a
necessity...John Muir*

Insights, thoughts and feelings:

Date:	Time:	Location & Trail Name:	Distance:
Weather: ☀ ⛅ 🌧 🌨	Type of Hike: Light Moderate Strenuous		Companions:

The sights, sounds, and smells of this hike:

_____
_____
_____
_____
_____
_____
_____
_____
_____
_____
_____

I have two doctors, my left leg and my right.
~ G.M. Trevelyan

Insights, thoughts and feelings:

Date:	Time:	Location & Trail Name:	Distance:
Weather: ☀ ⛅ 🌧 🌨	Type of Hike: Light Moderate Strenuous		Companions:

The sights, sounds, and smells of this hike:

_____

_____

_____

_____

_____

_____

_____

_____

_____

_____

_____

_____

Take care of your body. It's the only place you have to live.

~Jim Rohn

Insights, thoughts and feelings:

Date:	Time:	Location & Trail Name:	Distance:
Weather: ☀ ⛅ 🌧 🌨	Type of Hike: Light Moderate Strenuous		Companions:

The sights, sounds, and smells of this hike:

_____

_____

_____

_____

_____

_____

_____

_____

_____

_____

Nothing is more beautiful than the loveliness of the woods before sunrise.

~George Washington Carver

Insights, thoughts and feelings:

Date:	Time:	Location & Trail Name:	Distance:
Weather: ☀ ⛅ 🌧 🌨	Type of Hike: Light Moderate Strenuous		Companions:

The sights, sounds, and smells of this hike:

_____

_____

_____

_____

_____

_____

_____

_____

_____

_____

May your search through Nature lead you to
yourself.

~Author Unknown

Insights, thoughts and feelings:

Date:	Time:	Location & Trail Name:	Distance:
Weather: ☀ ⛅ 🌧 🌨	Type of Hike: Light Moderate Strenuous		Companions:

The sights, sounds, and smells of this hike:

_____

_____

_____

_____

_____

_____

_____

_____

_____

_____

_____

> *The farther one gets into the wilderness, the greater is*
> *the attraction of its lonely freedom.*
>
> *~Theodore Roosevelt*

Insights, thoughts and feelings:

Date:	Time:	Location & Trail Name:	Distance:
Weather: ☀ ⛅ 🌧 🌨	Type of Hike: Light Moderate Strenuous		Companions:

The sights, sounds, and smells of this hike:

_____

_____

_____

_____

_____

_____

_____

_____

_____

_____

*You have succeeded in life when all you really want
is only what you really need.*

~Vernon Howard

Insights, thoughts and feelings:

Date:	Time:	Location & Trail Name:	Distance:
Weather: ☀ ⛅ 🌧 🌨	Type of Hike: Light Moderate Strenuous		Companions:

The sights, sounds, and smells of this hike:

_____

_____

_____

_____

_____

_____

_____

_____

_____

_____

_____

The greatest step towards a life of simplicity is to learn to let go.

~Steve Maraboli

Insights, thoughts and feelings:

Date:	Time:	Location & Trail Name:	Distance:
Weather: ☀ ⛅ 🌧 🌨	Type of Hike: Light Moderate Strenuous		Companions:

The sights, sounds, and smells of this hike:

_____

_____

_____

_____

_____

_____

_____

_____

_____

_____

_____

> *There is no telling how many miles you will have to run while chasing a dream.*
>
> *~Author Unknown*

Insights, thoughts and feelings:

Date:	Time:	Location & Trail Name:	Distance:
Weather: ☀ ⛅ 🌧 🌨	Type of Hike: Light Moderate Strenuous		Companions:

The sights, sounds, and smells of this hike:

_____

_____

_____

_____

_____

_____

_____

_____

_____

_____

_____

I may not be there yet, but I'm closer than I was yesterday.

~Author Unknown

Insights, thoughts and feelings:

Date:	Time:	Location & Trail Name:	Distance:
Weather: ☀ ⛅ 🌧 🌨	Type of Hike: Light Moderate Strenuous		Companions:

The sights, sounds, and smells of this hike:

_____

_____

_____

_____

_____

_____

_____

_____

_____

_____

Those at the top of the mountain didn't fall there.

~Author Unknown

Insights, thoughts and feelings:

Date:	Time:	Location & Trail Name:	Distance:
Weather: ☀ ⛅ 🌧 🌨	Type of Hike: Light Moderate Strenuous		Companions:

The sights, sounds, and smells of this hike:

_____

_____

_____

_____

_____

_____

_____

_____

_____

_____

The view is better when it is earned.

~Author Unknown

Insights, thoughts and feelings:

Date:	Time:	Location & Trail Name:	Distance:
Weather:	Type of Hike:		Companions:

Weather: ☀ ⛅ 🌧 🌨

Type of Hike:

Light   Moderate   Strenuous

The sights, sounds, and smells of this hike:

_____

_____

_____

_____

_____

_____

_____

_____

_____

_____

_____

> *Walking takes longer... than any other known form of locomotion except crawling. Thus it stretches time and prolongs life. Life is already too short to waste on speed.*
>
> *~ Edward Abbey, "Walking"*

Insights, thoughts and feelings:

Date:	Time:	Location & Trail Name:	Distance:
Weather: ☀ ⛅ 🌧 🌨	Type of Hike: Light Moderate Strenuous		Companions:

The sights, sounds, and smells of this hike:

_____

_____

_____

_____

_____

_____

_____

_____

_____

_____

A vigorous five-mile walk will do more good for an unhappy but otherwise healthy adult than all the medicine and psychology in the world.

~ Paul Dudley White

Insights, thoughts and feelings:

Date:	Time:	Location & Trail Name:	Distance:
Weather: ☀ ⛅ 🌧 🌨	Type of Hike: Light Moderate Strenuous		Companions:

The sights, sounds, and smells of this hike:

_____

_____

_____

_____

_____

_____

_____

_____

_____

_____

_____

We ought to take outdoor walks, to refresh and raise
our spirits by deep breathing in the open air.

~ Lucius Annaeus Seneca

Insights, thoughts and feelings:

Date:	Time:	Location & Trail Name:	Distance:
Weather: ☀ ⛅ 🌧 🌨	Type of Hike: Light Moderate Strenuous		Companions:

The sights, sounds, and smells of this hike:

_____

_____

_____

_____

_____

_____

_____

_____

_____

_____

_____

> *It is not easy to walk alone in the country without musing upon something.*
>
> *~Charles Dickens*

Insights, thoughts and feelings:

Date:	Time:	Location & Trail Name:	Distance:
Weather: ☀ ⛅ 🌧 🌨	Type of Hike: Light Moderate Strenuous		Companions:

The sights, sounds, and smells of this hike:

_____

_____

_____

_____

_____

_____

_____

_____

_____

_____

_____

All truly great thoughts are conceived by walking.

~Friedrich Nietzsche

Insights, thoughts and feelings:

Date:	Time:	Location & Trail Name:	Distance:
Weather: ☀ ⛅ ☁ ☁	Type of Hike: Light Moderate Strenuous		Companions:

The sights, sounds, and smells of this hike:

_____

_____

_____

_____

_____

_____

_____

_____

_____

_____

_____

> *In every walk with nature one receives far more*
> *than he seeks.*
>
> *~ John Muir*

Insights, thoughts and feelings:

Date:	Time:	Location & Trail Name:	Distance:
Weather: ☀ ⛅ ☔ ☃	Type of Hike: Light Moderate Strenuous		Companions:

The sights, sounds, and smells of this hike:

_____

_____

_____

_____

_____

_____

_____

_____

_____

_____

_____

All walking is discovery. On foot we take the time to see things whole.

~ Hal Borland

Insights, thoughts and feelings:

Date:	Time:	Location & Trail Name:	Distance:
Weather:	Type of Hike:		Companions:

Weather: ☀ ⛅ 🌧 🌨

Type of Hike:

Light   Moderate   Strenuous

The sights, sounds, and smells of this hike:

_____

_____

_____

_____

_____

_____

_____

_____

_____

_____

Walking is a man's best medicine.

- Hippocrates

Insights, thoughts and feelings:

Date:	Time:	Location & Trail Name:	Distance:
Weather: ☀ ⛅ 🌧 🌨	Type of Hike: Light Moderate Strenuous		Companions:

The sights, sounds, and smells of this hike:

_____

_____

_____

_____

_____

_____

_____

_____

_____

_____

_____

> *When you walk in the mountains stands of cedar, among the wise old elder trees, anything you want to know you can find there.*
>
> *- Saying of the Lummi Tribe of Puget Sound*

Insights, thoughts and feelings:

Date:	Time:	Location & Trail Name:	Distance:
Weather:	Type of Hike:		Companions:

Weather:
☀ ⛅
🌧 🌨

Type of Hike:
Light   Moderate   Strenuous

Companions:

The sights, sounds, and smells of this hike:

_____

_____

_____

_____

_____

_____

_____

_____

_____

_____

> *Walking would teach people the quality that*
> *youngsters find so hard to learn - patience.*
>
> *- Edward P. Weston*

Insights, thoughts and feelings:

Date:	Time:	Location & Trail Name:	Distance:
Weather: ☀ ⛅ 🌧 🌨	Type of Hike: Light Moderate Strenuous		Companions:

The sights, sounds, and smells of this hike:

_____

_____

_____

_____

_____

_____

_____

_____

_____

_____

_____

*Hiking is the best workout! ... You can hike for three hours
and not even realize you're working out. And, hiking
alone lets me have some time to myself.*

~ Jamie Luner

Insights, thoughts and feelings:

Date:	Time:	Location & Trail Name:	Distance:
Weather: ☀ ⛅ 🌧 🌨	Type of Hike: Light Moderate Strenuous		Companions:

The sights, sounds, and smells of this hike:

_____

_____

_____

_____

_____

_____

_____

_____

_____

_____

_____

As you sit on the hillside, or lie prone under the trees of the forest, or sprawl wet-legged by a mountain stream, the great door, that does not look like a door, opens.

- Stephen Graham

Insights, thoughts and feelings:

Date:	Time:	Location & Trail Name:	Distance:
Weather: ☀ ⛅ 🌧 🌨	Type of Hike: Light Moderate Strenuous		Companions:

The sights, sounds, and smells of this hike:

_____

_____

_____

_____

_____

_____

_____

_____

_____

_____

Few people know how to take a walk. The qualifications are endurance, plain clothes, old shoes, an eye for nature, good humor, vast curiosity, good speech, good silence and nothing too much. ~ Ralph Waldo Emerson

Insights, thoughts and feelings:

Date:	Time:	Location & Trail Name:	Distance:
Weather: ☀ ⛅ 🌧 🌨	Type of Hike: Light Moderate Strenuous		Companions:

The sights, sounds, and smells of this hike:

_____

_____

_____

_____

_____

_____

_____

_____

_____

_____

_____

If you are walking to seek, ye shall find."

- Sommeil Liberosensa

Insights, thoughts and feelings:

Date:	Time:	Location & Trail Name:	Distance:
Weather: ☀ ⛅ 🌧 🌨	Type of Hike: Light Moderate Strenuous		Companions:

The sights, sounds, and smells of this hike:

_____

_____

_____

_____

_____

_____

_____

_____

_____

_____

_____

Everywhere is walking distance if you have the time.

~Steven Wright

Insights, thoughts and feelings:

Date:	Time:	Location & Trail Name:	Distance:
Weather: ☀ ⛅ 🌧 🌨	Type of Hike: Light Moderate Strenuous		Companions:

The sights, sounds, and smells of this hike:

_____

_____

_____

_____

_____

_____

_____

_____

_____

_____

*Remember that time spent on a rock climb isn't
subtracted from your life span."*

~ Will Niccolls

Insights, thoughts and feelings:

Date:	Time:	Location & Trail Name:	Distance:
Weather: ☀ ⛅ 🌧 🌨	Type of Hike: Light Moderate Strenuous		Companions:

The sights, sounds, and smells of this hike:

_____

_____

_____

_____

_____

_____

_____

_____

_____

_____

_____

He who limps is still walking.

~Stanislaw J. Lec

Insights, thoughts and feelings:

Date:	Time:	Location & Trail Name:	Distance:
Weather:	Type of Hike: Light Moderate Strenuous		Companions:

The sights, sounds, and smells of this hike:

_____

_____

_____

_____

_____

_____

_____

_____

_____

_____

_____

Now shall I walk or shall I ride?
"Ride," Pleasure said:
"Walk," Joy replied.
~W.H. Davies

Insights, thoughts and feelings:

If you enjoyed this journal, we have many more styles and types to choose from. Visit our website for a complete list of journals.

www.wanderingwalksofwonder.com

Baseball Stadium Exploration Journal

National Parks Exploration Journal

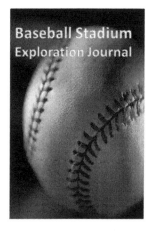

My Bucket List Journal

Lighthouse Exploration Journal

43064288R00068

Made in the USA
Lexington, KY
16 July 2015